DRAMA START TWO

Drama Activities and Plays for Children
(Ages 9-12)

First published in 2012 by
JemBooks
Montenotte,
Cork,
Ireland
www.jembooks.ie

ISBN: 978-0-9568966-1-2

Typesetting by Gough Typesetting Service, Dublin

DRAMA START TWO

DRAMA ACTIVITIES AND PLAYS CHILDREN
(AGES 9-12)

Julie Meighan

JemBooks

About the Author

Julie Meighan is a lecturer in Drama in Education at the Cork Institute of Technology. She has taught Drama to all age groups and levels. She is the author of *Drama Start: Drama Activities, Plays and Monologues for Young Children (ages 3 -8)*. ISBN 978-0956896605.

Drama Start 2 is a collection of drama activities and plays suitable for children between the ages of nine and twelve. This book is also suitable for anyone working with children in a setting where drama is used, such as community groups, out-of-school care facilities, therapeutic group work and so on.

The book is accessible and easy to follow. It is divided into two parts:

     Part 1 – Drama Games
     Part 2 – Plays

Each section provides educators/leaders with a variety of creative and imaginative ideas to stimulate drama activities in many different settings.

Contents

PART ONE: DRAMA GAMES

Warm-ups Games

Relaxation Games

Articulation Games

Mime and Movement Games

Communication Games

Concentration Games

Storytelling Games

Improvisation Games

PART TWO: PLAYS FOR CHILDREN

Part One: Drama Games

Drama games are a perfect tool to use in any classroom that encompasses multiple learning styles, ability levels and age groups. They facilitate children's ability to learn in different ways as visual learners, auditory learners and kinaesthetic learners. The games help improve self-confidence, build trust and develop creativity, but they can also have a profound effect on literary development, academic success and social interaction. The games help children to explore creative drama, mime, movement and storytelling. The activities are fun, challenging and rewarding, not only for the students but also for the educators/leaders themselves.

This book can be used by anyone working with children so I have called the person who is running the group the leader.

Some Important Advice for Leaders Before You Begin

- Start with very simple games that the children may already know, such as *What is the time, Mr Wolf?* Once you have built a sense of trust and teamwork, begin to focus on more complex and exploratory games or on games that demand a child's involvement.

- Never ask a group to play a game that you would not play yourself.

- Watch the language used – avoid terms like play or games and instead use words like focus, explore, challenge and participate.

- Be very clear with your instructions. Ask for feedback from the students to make sure they understand what is involved and what each participant has to do.

- Be enthusiastic. The children will be drawn to your energy and will get excited about the prospect of participating in the activity.

- Give a demonstration wherever possible.

- Involve yourself in the game. Don't give the group instructions and then go and sit in a corner of the room, just watching or correcting.

Each Drama Game is listed with details of the minimum number of children required for the game to work. Detailed instructions are also provided with suggested variations for some of the games. The resources needed are included and the difficulty of each game is described using the star rating system below:

*	Very Easy
**	Easy
***	Medium
****	Difficult
*****	Very Difficult

Warm-ups Games

Warm-ups games are very important and beneficial for any drama class
– no matter what age:

- They are fun and enjoyable.
- They help the children get to know one another.
- They help children focus on the drama class that follows the
  warm-up.
- They help the children limber-up.
- They help shy children to get involved in the group.
- They help children to use their imagination and creativity.
- They promote trust among the children.

Game: Orders
Difficulty rating: **
Minimum number of participants: 6
Resources needed: Clear space
Instructions: This warm-up game helps children to learn how to work as a team. The leader tells everyone to get into a straight line and not to make a sound or move their mouths throughout the game; they can only communicate through the use of non-verbal body language.

When the instructions have been given, the leader asks the group to get in a straight line in some order, e.g. the leader can ask them to line-up from the oldest to the youngest. If too many children were born in the same month, they can progress to finding out what day they were born and line-up in that order; or they can get in order according to height, alphabetically by first names, or if any have the same first names, they can get in line alphabetically by their surnames.

They have to complete the task communicating through non-verbal language such as pointing, miming etc. When the line is completed the leader asks each child to tell him/her their name or age. Then they can see if they managed to communicate their message through non-verbal language. This can take some time and a lot of concentration. It is also a good way for the leader and the class to learn each other's names.

Game: Crossing the circle
Difficulty rating: *
Minimum number of participants: 6
Resources needed: Clear space
Instructions: The children stand in a circle and the leader gives everyone a number from 1 to 3. Then the leader tells all the 1s to exchange places by crossing the circle; and then all the 2s to cross the circle and so on. When the children understand what to do, the leader calls out different ways for them to walk across the circle:

> Like a toddler
> Like a frail old man
> Like a lion
> Like a mouse
> Like a roller blade
> Like a ballerina
> Like Justin Timberlake/Justin Bieber
> Like a rock star
> Like a princess
> Like Superman
> Like a rally car

Game: Prisoner
Difficulty rating: *
Minimum number of participants: 4
Resources needed: A large space, chairs
Instructions: Divide the group into pairs. One is the prisoner and the other is the jailer. All the prisoners sit in chairs in a circle while all the jailers stand behind their prisoner with their backs to the chairs. The leader sits in the circle with the prisoners, but does not have a jailer. When the leader shouts a prisoner's name, they must change places with another prisoner as quickly as possible. However, if the jailer turns around fast enough and taps the prisoner on the shoulder, the prisoner is caught and can't move. The leader then calls out someone else's name. This is an excellent warm-up game, but it also helps with reflexes and listening skills.

Game: Pass the shake
Difficulty rating: **
Minimum number of participants: 4
Resources needed: Clear space
Instructions: The children stand in a circle and one child volunteers to start. S/He then begins to shake a part of his/her body, for example hand, leg or head and then makes eye contact with someone else in the circle. S/He throws the shake to that child. The other child catches it, comes up with his/her own shake and begins to move that part of his/her body. Then s/he makes eye contact with another child and throws him/her the shake. The game continues until everyone in the circle has had a chance to shake something. Each child must shake a different part of his body, so it gets more difficult as the game goes on. This is an excellent activity for developing observation and co-operation skills.

Game: Magic chairs
Difficulty rating: *
Minimum number of participants: 2
Resources needed: Clear space, one chair per child
Instructions: Ask each member of the group to get a chair and choose a place to put it. They then have to walk a few steps away from their chair. The leader can change the chair into whatever she wants. If she calls out "highchair," the children must walk back to their chairs and climb into them as if they were highchairs.

Types of chairs that could be called out include:

A throne
A toilet seat
A seat in a crowded bus
A dentist's chair
A chair with chewing gum on it
A chair with a mouse on it
A wet chair
A rocking chair
A lounger that is very hot from being out in the sun
A chair with a whoopee cushion
A slippery chair
A spinning chair

Game: Circle of chairs
Difficulty rating: *
Minimum number of participants: 5
Resources needed: Clear space, one chair per child
Instructions: All the children sit in chairs in a circle. One child volunteers to stand in the middle. When the child in the middle starts walking back towards the empty chair, the other children must try to stop him/her by sitting on it. Then the child in the middle walks towards another free chair, and the other children must try to prevent him/her from sitting on that one as well. This activity can get out of hand, so it is important to include some rules such as walking only; no running. Try to get the children to fool each other using body language and eye contact.

Game: Three legs, two heads and a nose
Difficulty rating: ***
Minimum number of participants: 3
Resources needed: Clear space
Instructions: Divide the class into groups of three. The leader explains that each group must try to join together in some way. Then the leader calls out parts of the body. The children must arrange themselves so that only those parts of their bodies can be touching the ground. For example, three legs, two heads and a nose, or three knees, two hands and a leg. If a group falls over or if they have more parts of the body touching the ground than have been called out, then that group is out.

This fun game helps not only with movement but also encourages imagination and teamwork. The leader may have to write the instructions on the board to make it easier for the children to follow.

Game: Thank you for using me
Difficulty rating: ***
Minimum number of participants: 3
Resources needed: Clear space
Instructions: Everyone sits in a circle and one child volunteers to stand in the centre. S/He makes a shape with his/her body. Then a second child enters the circle, looks at the shape and thinks of an object that can be used with the shape. S/He then pretends to use the object. The rest of the group has to guess the object. When the rest of the group guess correctly the first child leaves the circle; the second child makes a shape and then a third child comes into the circle, looks at the second child's shape, decides on an object and mimes using it. The leader should suggest to the children that they just make a shape and don't try to be a certain object. It is up to the child who enters the circle to use his/her imagination to decide what the other child's shape is supposed to depict.

Game: The name game
Difficulty rating: *
Minimum number of participants: 3
Resources needed: Clear space
Instructions: This is an excellent warm-up game but it is also very useful if the class doesn't know one another very well. The class stands in a circle and the leader throws a ball to a child. That child must then introduce her/himself to the rest of the group. However, the child must also say a word that describes her/him and that starts with the same letter as her/his name.

> Examples:
> Hi, I'm awesome Andrew;
> Hi, I'm beautiful Betty;
> Hi, I'm careful Cathy;
> And so on.

Game: Getting to know you
Difficulty rating: *
Minimum number of participants: 4
Resources needed: Clear space
Instructions: Divide the group into pairs. Each pair speaks to each other for five minutes. They must find out five things about their partner that they didn't know before the start of the conversation. When the five minutes are up, the pair return to the group and tell them the five things they have learned about their partner. This is a good 'getting-to-know-you' activity for children who don't know each other. However this activity works quite effectively if the group is familiar with one another; they just have to use their imaginations.

Relaxation Games

Relaxation is very important in Drama. The following activities will enable children to reduce stress and to help them release mental, physical and emotional tension. A relaxed body also leads to good voice production – benefiting all aspects of the voice such as pitch, pace, pause, inflection and projection.

Game: Be a waxwork
Difficulty rating: *
Minimum number of participants: 2
Resources needed: Clear space
Instructions: The children must imagine that they are a waxwork in Madame Tussauds' Museum in London. Everyone can decide which very famous person they want to be. The children get into position and then the leader walks around looking at the waxworks and tries to guess who is who. When she has guessed everyone there is unfortunately a fire in the museum and all the waxworks melt slowly to the ground.

Game: Smoke in the chimney
Difficulty rating: *
Minimum number of participants: 2
Resources needed: Clear space
Instructions: The children imagine that they are smoke rising up from a chimney. They move, undulating slowly. They stretch their bodies as much as they can and then they finally relax.

Game: Puppet on a string
Difficulty rating: ***
Minimum number of participants: 2
Resources needed: Clear space
Instructions: The children imagine they are puppets with strings attached to their shoulders that someone is pulling from above. The leader tells them that they are being pulled up and their limbs fly out in all directions. Even the feet can be pulled off the ground at times. Finally the strings are cut, and the body relaxes.

Game: Floating tongue
Difficulty rating: *
Minimum number of participants: 1 (and the Leader)
Resources needed: Clear space
Instructions: The children are told to hold their tongues out of their mouths. They have to make sure that their tongues don't touch any part of the mouth. Then the leader tells them to clench their jaws and relax them slowly. After that they let their tongues completely relax. They should do this five times.

Game: Lion's roar
Difficulty rating: *
Minimum number of participants: 1
Resources needed: Clear space
Instructions: Each child imagines that s/he is a mighty lion with a loud roar. But the roar is bottled up inside the lion. S/he should stand up like a proud lion; scrunch up his/her face and hands, ready to let the lion's roar go. Then the leader tells them to take a deep breath and let the roar out. Tell them to stick out their tongues and hold their arms and hands out in front of them as they roar.

Game: The rock
Difficulty rating: **
Minimum number of participants: 1 (and the Leader)
Resources needed: Clear space and chairs
Instructions: Each child sits on a chair with knees bent, feet firmly on the ground and back straight. The leader tells them they are rocks embedded in the sea. They should feel the cool and refreshing sea water against them. Tell them to take a deep breath of sea air and let it go gently, imagining the sound of seagulls in the distance. Tell them to breathe in and out slowly and gently, feeling each breath with their whole body. When their bodies are completely relaxed, gently tell them to slowly open their eyes. Have them discuss how this felt.

Game: Happy place
Difficulty rating: ***
Minimum number of participants: 1 (and the Leader)
Resources needed: Clear space, mats
Instructions: The children should lie down on mats and close their eyes. Tell them to imagine they are in a place where they feel happy and safe. Tell them to think about: what they see; what they hear. Tell them in their happy place they should feel safe, peaceful and relaxed. Tell them to put their left hand on top of their right hand and that when they do this in future, they will go back to their happy place. Then gently ask them to slowly open their eyes.

Articulation Games

These games will help to improve the children's fluency with language. They also help to improve clarity of speech sounds and assist with vocal projection.

Game: Voice coach
Difficulty rating: **
Minimum number of participants: 2
Resources needed: Clear space, index cards with emotions written on them
Instructions: Choose a simple sentence, e.g. "I want a can of Coke." Write one of the feelings listed below on each index card. Have one child choose a card and then say the simple sentence in the emotion written on it. The rest of the class has to guess which emotion the child is trying to portray.

Examples of emotions which can be used:
    Calm
    Happy
    Sad
    Stubborn
    Surprised
    Excited
    Angry
    Worried
    Brave
    Lonely

At the end, have the children repeat the sentence together, as they all use the emotion they have chosen from the card.

Game: Different strokes
Difficulty rating: **
Minimum number of participants: 8
Resources needed: Clear space
Instructions: The leader makes a simple statement such as "I like walking in summer" or "Maths homework is difficult" in different ways. For example as if:

    o They are talking to a toddler.
    o They are shouting across the playground.
    o They are bored of saying it so many times.
    o They are coming around after an operation.

Game: Tongue-twisters
Difficulty rating: * to *****
Minimum number of participants: 1
Resources needed: Handouts with tongue twisters on them
Instructions: The children must start slowly and articulate each word clearly. They can go faster and faster as they feel more confident with the tongue twisters. If you have a large class, divide them into groups of four or five.

Some sample tongue-twisters to help you get started:
A skunk sat on a stump. The stump thought the skunk stunk. The skunk thought the stump stunk. What stunk? The skunk or the stump?
A tutor who tooted the flute, tried to tutor two tooters to toot; said the two tooters to the tutor: "Is it harder to toot or to tutor two tooters to toot?"
If Freaky Fred found fifty feet of fruit and fed forty feet to his friend Frank, how many feet of fruit did Freaky Fred find?
Pepperoni pizza on a pink-patterned plate with parsley on the side to your pleasure.
Peter Piper picked a peck of pickled peppers. If Peter Piper picked a peck of pickled peppers; where's the peck of pickled peppers Peter Piper picked?
Red Leather Yellow Leather Red Leather Yellow Leather Red Leather Yellow Leather...
She shut the shop shutters so the shopping shoppers can't shop.
Unique New York; Unique New York; Unique New York ...
Which wristwatch is a Swiss wristwatch?
I like New York, unique New York, I like unique New York.
Peggy Babcock loves Tubby Gigwhip.
Two toads totally tired, tried to trot to Tewkesbury.
She stood upon the balcony, inimitably mimicking him hiccupping and amicably welcoming him in.
The sixth sick Sheik's sixth sheep's sick.

Betty Botter bought some butter
But she said, "This butter's bitter.
But a bit of better butter's
Better than the bitter butter,
That would make my batter better."
So she bought some better butter
Better than the bitter butter
And it made her batter better.
So 'twas better Betty Botter,
Bought a bit of better butter.

Game: Broken telephone
Difficulty rating: **
Minimum number of participants: 5
Resources needed: Clear space, chairs/mats
Instructions: This is a classic game. With the class sitting in a circle, the leader whispers a simple message to one of the children. They must pass the message on to the child next to them, but they must follow a few rules. They must whisper but still speak clearly. They can say the message only once. When everyone in the circle has passed the message to the child next to them, the last child stands up and repeats the message they heard. The message has usually changed along the way, so the leader then tries to find out which children are 'broken telephones' as the 'telephone' may be broken in more than one place!

Tongues-twisters can be very effective messages to use here as they help children to be careful with their articulation.

Some examples to help you get started:
She sells sea shells at the seashore.
Four fat frogs fanning fainting flies.
Round the rock the ragged rascal ran.

Game: Stand back – the bridge is breaking
Difficulty rating: *
Minimum number of participants: 2
Resources needed: Handouts of the poem
Instructions: The children each receive a copy of the poem below. They must read it out, making sure they recite it really quietly when the writing is very small. Then they get louder and louder as the writing gets bigger and bigger, until finally they are projecting their voices as loudly as they can.

> *Pitter-patter, drops of rain*
> *Tapping on the window pane*
>
> *Now the rain is coming down*
> *On all the houses in the town*
> *Beating, battering shops and shutters*
> *Hurling leaves into the gutters.*
>
> *Wildly lashing streets and fields,*
> *Pelting rain and stormy seas*
> *The river roars, the bridge is shaking,*
> *Stand back, stand back, the bridge is BREAKING.*

Game: Gibberish
Difficulty rating: ****
Minimum number of participants: 4
Resources needed: Clear space, index cards listing different situations
Instructions: Divide the group into pairs. Each pair chooses an index card that gives them a context for their conversation, see examples below. They then have to act out the situation but they can't use actual words, instead they replace the words with letters of the alphabet. To get their situation across, they must focus on their tone, pitch, inflection, projection and pace to communicate their situation. The rest of the group have to guess the context of the pair's conversation and what is happening.

Some examples of different situations:
In a restaurant (waiter and customer) – customer complaining about the food.

At a hairdresser (hairdresser and customer) – customer trying to hide her disappointment about her haircut.

Under the moonlight (boyfriend and girlfriend) – he tells her he loves her.

Game: Sound spy
Difficulty rating: *
Minimum number of participants: 2
Resources needed: Clear space
Instructions: This is based on the traditional game of 'I Spy' but in this version, the children must look for something that has a sound. For example: I sound spy with my little eye something that starts with the sound 'D'. It could be a number of things like a desk, a door or a dress. To make things more difficult, the children could say I spy with my little eye something that finishes with the sound 'S'. It could be a variety of things like keys, pens or windows.

Game: Big balloon
Difficulty rating: **
Minimum number of participants: 1 (and the Leader)
Resources needed: Clear space.
Instructions: Each child must imagine that they have a balloon. They must blow it up and hold it at the end. Tell them that every time they breathe, they are pushing the balloon farther and farther away, until finally it glides into the sky.

Game: Secret voices
Difficulty rating: ***
Minimum number of participants: 4
Resources needed: Clear space, blindfold
Instructions: One of the children volunteers to be blindfolded. Everyone else is given 15 seconds to find a place in the room where they must all stand still. The leader points to one of the children, who are all standing still, and that child disguises his/her voice by changing pitch and tone and asks: "Do you know who I am?" If the blindfolded volunteer guesses correctly, s/he gets to choose the next child to be blindfolded. If s/he guesses incorrectly, the leader keeps picking children until the blindfolded child guesses correctly.

Game: Vocal projection
Difficulty rating: ****
Minimum number of participants: 2
Resources needed: Clear space
Instructions: Divide the group into pairs. One child in the pair talks about a topic such as holidays, sports, TV, school, and so on; the other child listens and after a few seconds says "louder." Eventually the child talking will be shouting. After three or four times of saying "louder," the listener can start saying "softer". The listener can also go back and forth between "louder" and "softer" as s/he wants. This fun game leads to lots of laughs.

Game: Sound nursery rhymes
Difficulty rating: ****
Minimum number of participants: 8
Resources needed: Clear space
Instructions: Divide the participants into groups of four or five. Each group must choose a nursery rhyme between them and come up with a way of expressing that nursery rhyme just by using their bodies to make sounds for example stamping feet, slapping knees or clapping hands. They cannot speak or make any sounds with their mouth. They must perform for the other groups, who must then try to guess the nursery rhyme.

Mime and Movement Games

Movement is about expressing yourself physically. The movement games below improve a child's flexibility, co-ordination, balance and control. The games are also an excellent way for children to explore body language, by practising and observing, and also to learn how to walk like a specific character.

Mime is an integral part of Drama and the activities in this section enable the children to improve their mime skills. Children often find mine easier because they don't have to speak.

Game: Movement sequences
Difficulty rating: *
Minimum number of participants: 2
Resources needed: Large space
Instructions: The leader talks to the children about different ways of moving. Ask them to call out different ways people move.

Examples to get you started include:

- o walking
- o running
- o crawling
- o rolling
- o hopping
- o skipping
- o jumping
- o leaping
- o tiptoeing
- o tumbling
- o turning
- o galloping
- o twirling
- o spinning
- o walking sideways
- o walking backwards

The children will come up with many more. When they have moved in all the different ways, the leader calls out movement sequences such as:

- o walk – jump – twirl – tumble
- o spin – hop – skip – gallop

Give the children a chance to be the leader and to call out their own movement sequences.

Game: Walk on the wild side
Difficulty rating: *
Minimum number of participants: 2
Resources needed: Clear space
Instructions: Ask the students to think about the ways people walk. Then ask them to walk around the room as you call out different ways of walking.

Examples to get you started include walk like a:

- o toddler;
- o child in high heels
- o child wearing heavy Wellington boots
- o child splashing in a puddles
- o child stuck in mud
- o child on stony beach
- o child on hot sand
- o someone on fire
- o someone wearily
- o an old frail person

Game: The 10-second machines
Difficulty rating: ***
Minimum number of participants: 5
Resources needed: Clear space
Instructions: Divide the class into groups of five. The leader calls out a machine and the group has 10 seconds to make that object, using their five bodies. Each child in the group has to be part of the machine.

Examples of machines:

- o dishwasher
- o television
- o radio
- o fridge
- o car
- o tractor
- o train
- o photocopier
- o computer

Game: Sculptor at work
Difficulty rating: ****
Minimum number of participants: 8
Resources needed: Clear Space
Instructions: Divide the class into pairs. One child in each pair will be the clay and the other is the sculptor. The sculptor is going to mould the 'clay' into a shape. The leader decides on the theme s/he wants them to use.

For example:

- o how I feel today
- o how I feel at this moment
- o my favourite TV character
- o my favourite book character

The entire class looks at each sculpture and tries to guess what it is. When they have completed this, the students in each pair switch roles and start again.

Extension: Divide the class into small groups. Each group chooses a sculptor; then they have to create a sculpture of:

- o their favourite memory
- o an embarrassing moment
- o a surprising moment
- o a sad moment
- o a happy moment

Game: Five ways in 20 seconds
Difficulty rating: ***
Minimum number of participants: 4 or 5
Resources needed: Clear space
Instructions: In groups of four or five, the children must come up with five ways of showing that they are:

- o cold
- o hot
- o hungry
- o shocked
- o frightened

Each group must show the rest of the class their five different mimes in 20 seconds. The leader counts to 20 for each group's turn so the children in each group have to be quick and work as a team.

Game: Chain mime
Difficulty rating: ****
Minimum number of participants: 8
Resources needed: Clear space
Instructions: Divide the class into two groups. Each child in for example Group A numbers themselves from one to 10, or up to however many children are in the group. Then ask all of Group A to leave the room except for child Number 1. When the rest of the group have left, the leader explains that they are going to do a simple mime for child Number 2. When child Number 2 comes back into the room s/he watches the mime but can't guess what it's about. Number 2 then mimes it for child Number 3 when s/he comes into the room. Number 3 watches and then repeats the mine for Child Number 4 and so on until the last child in the group has to guess the mime. Only the last person in the group can guess. Then child Number 1 does the original mime for everyone so they can see where they want wrong.

All this time Group B is in the room looking at what is happening and where mistakes are being made. When Group A is finished, it is Group B's turn to leave the room.

Examples of some simple mimes:

- o brushing your teeth
- o sending a text message
- o washing the dog
- o riding a horse
- o baking a cake
- o doing the washing-up

Game: Meetings
Difficulty rating: **
Minimum number of participants: 2
Resources needed: Clear space
Instructions: Divide the children into pairs and tell them to stand back-to-back. When the leader counts to three, they turn around and greet each other, trying out different scenarios.

Children mime meeting:

- o as if they are strangers
- o as if they are casual acquaintances
- o someone they haven't seen for years
- o someone they don't like
- o someone who owes them a lot of money

Game: Fairy tales' charade relay
Difficulty rating: ***
Minimum number of participants: 8
Resources needed: Clear space, two sets of identical cards with the names of fairy tales on them.
Instructions: This is based on the popular game charades but with a twist. Divide the class into two groups. Each group numbers themselves from 1 to 10 or however many children are in the group. The leader has two identical sets of cards. On each card is the name of a fairy-tale character. The cards for each group are in the same order. When the leader says "Go," child Number 1 has to try to communicate the first fairy-tale character to child Number 2, without speaking. Number 1 can use his/her fingers to tell child Number 2 the number of words or can mime that it "sounds like". Number 2 is the only child who can guess; the rest of the group has to be quiet even if they know the answer. When Number 2 guesses correctly, s/he runs to the leader to get the second card. Number 2 looks at the next character and mimes that to Number 3, who again is the only child who can guess.

This goes on until one group has gone through all the cards are declared the winners. If someone blurts out the answer out of turn, his/her group incurs penalty points or has to do an extra mime.

Some examples of fairy-tale characters:

o Little Red Riding Hood
o Grandmother
o The ugly Stepsisters
o Wicked Queen
o The Witch
o Snow White
o Cinderella
o The Gingerbread Man
o The Little Red Hen
o Chicken Lickin
o The Wicked Wolf

Variation: The leader can substitute fairy-tale characters with book characters or TV characters. I use fairy-tale characters because most children are familiar with them.

Game: Bus stop
Difficulty rating: ****
Minimum number of participants: 6
Resources needed: Clear space, index cards listing different characteristics
Instructions: The leader writes personality characteristics on the index cards and the children choose one each. Then they must walk up, wait at the bus stop and react as their character would in the same situation.

Examples of situations:

- o the bus is late
- o the bus comes but it breaks down
- o they wait a long time and then it begins to rain
- o a car splashes them
- o Two buses come together – how do they get on the right bus?

The rest of the class must guess what characteristic each individual was demonstrating.

Some characteristics that could be used include:

- o stubborn
- o excited
- o cranky
- o annoyed
- o happy
- o depressed
- o cruel
- o kind
- o selfish
- o foolish
- o gentle

Game: Group Mime
Difficulty rating: ****
Minimum number of participants: 9
Resources needed: Large clear space
Instructions: Divide the class into three groups and give each group a copy of one of the mimes below. Give the children in each group about 10 minutes to prepare their mime. Then they must perform it for the other groups.

The Concert
Audience arrives for outdoor concert.
Band enters with different instruments.
Audience is very enthusiastic, claps, jumps up and down and waves hands in the air.
One person faints.Security arrives and removes him/her. No one takes any notice. Band plays on.
Girl gets up on the stage and tries to touch members of the group. Security removes her.
It starts to rain and after a while everyone goes away disappointed.

Hijack
Passengers board the aeroplane and are welcomed by the air hostess.
The plane takes off.
One hijacker takes over the plane and a second one holds up the passengers.
A passenger faints. This distracts the second hijacker and the pilot overcomes him/her.
Air hostess holds hijacker and handcuffs are put on.
Pilot overcomes the second hijacker and handcuffs him/her to the first hijacker.
All the passengers have a strong cup of tea/coffee and cheer the pilot, as s/he lands the aeroplane.

The Bank Robbery
Cashiers arrive to start a day's work, bored and yawning. They open up their desks and talk to each other.
People come in and walk up to the cashiers and deposit and withdraw money.
Suddenly two robbers rush in wearing masks.
The robbers make everyone lie on the floor. They hold up the bank clerks and make them hand over the money; the thieves stuff it in a bag.
One little, old lady trips up a robber, he falls and money spills out of the bag.
A security guard then grabs robbers and takes off their masks.

Extension: other ideas/themes for group mimes include Camping, The Circus, Christmas Morning and The Big Mistake.

Communication Games

Communication is a two-way process. It is extremely important in Drama that children develop their listening skills, turn-taking abilities and that they respond in a positive way to what is being communicated to them. The following activities help children to think quickly, listen and respond appropriately.

The communication activities below will also improve children's problem-solving skills.

Game: Guide dogs
Difficulty rating: ****
Minimum number of participants:4
Resources needed: Clear space, blindfold.
Instructions: Divide the group into pairs. One person in the pair closes her/his eyes and the other person is the guide dog. The dog takes the blind person around the room, making sure s/he doesn't bump into anything. The children cannot talk during this game. After a few minutes the process should be reversed.

This is a very useful trust exercise.

Game: Captain's coming
Difficulty rating: *
Minimum number of participants: 3
Resources needed: Clear space
Instructions: The leader or a child can be the captain. The captain calls out orders to the rest of the children who are the crew. If a child does not follow an order correctly, s/he is out.

Orders	*Action*
Bow	Run to the front of the space.
Stern	Run to the back of the space.
Port	Run to the left side of the space.
Starboard	Run to the right side of the space.
Man overboard	Lie on back and swim.
Submarines	Lie on back and stick one leg straight up.
Man the lifeboats	Find a partner, sit together and row!
Scrub the decks	Crouch down and pretend to clean the floor with their hands.
Climb the rigging	Pretend to climb a rope ladder.
Captain's coming	Salute and shout out: "Aye, aye, Captain."
Walk the plank	Walk in a perfectly straight line one foot exactly in front of the other with arms outstretched to the sides.
Captain's daughter	Everyone curtseys.
Hit the deck	Lie on stomachs.

Game: Freeze and change
Difficulty rating: ****
Minimum number of participants: 4
Resources needed: Clear space
Instructions: Two children volunteer to go to the centre of a circle. In an impromptu manner, they begin acting out a scene about anything. When the leader shouts "freeze," the children freeze and child Number 1 leaves the centre. Child Number 3 then enters the centre and starts a different scene with child Number 2. The game goes around the circle until everyone has a go.

Game: Balloon debate
Difficulty rating: *****
Minimum number of participants: 6
Resources needed: Clear space
Instructions: Divide the class into groups of six. Each child in the group chooses a hero. The hero could be a historical figure, a footballer, their grandmother or whoever they think is worthy of hero status. The leader tells them that the six heroes are in the group's balloon, but the balloon is too heavy and only one hero can survive, so every student must put forward a case explaining why their chosen hero should remain in the balloon. The rest of the class then has to vote on it. Do this for all the groups. Then have a final balloon debate with all the group winners until there is only one hero in the balloon.

Game: King's/Queen's throne
Difficulty rating: *
Minimum number of participants: 4
Resources needed: Clear space, chair
Instructions: One child volunteers to be the king/queen and sits in a chair. Each child in the group must go before the king/queen, bow and say one positive thing about him/her. When the children have all said something positive, the king/queen nominates someone else in the group to be king/queen and sit on the throne.

Game: Last people on Earth
Difficulty rating: *****
Minimum number of participants: 5
Resources needed: Clear space, handout with a list of names of the last people on Earth
Instructions: The children are divided into groups of 5 or less and given the following handout of the last people on Earth:

Occupation	Age	Sex	Information
Doctor	69	Male	He has cancer.
Nun	35	Female	She is very religious.
Construction worker	45	Male	He has no arms.
Musician	21	Male	He is blind since birth.
Baby	9 months	Female	She is an orphan.
Punk	19	Male	He has depression.
Teacher	67	Male	He has never married.
Actress	27	Female	She is a feminist.
IT Expert	31	Female	She has no social skills.
Social Worker	29	Male	He is a drug addict.

The leader explains that there has been a nuclear war and the people on the list are the only ones left on Earth. There is enough room and food for five of them to live for a year in a bunker, where they will be protected from radiation and will survive. Each group must decide which five they think should survive.

Give the groups 15 or 20 minutes to discuss the dilemma. Each group then presents their final five to the rest of the class. The audience can ask questions and challenge the group's choices.

Game: Get connected
Difficulty rating: ****
Minimum number of participants: 6
Resources needed: Clear space, rope
Instructions: Divide the group into pairs. One pair volunteers to be 'connected'. That pair is given a rope that they each hold and can't let go of. The other children in the class use their bodies to make obstacles around the pair. The connected pair has to go through, under or over each obstacle, without letting go of the rope. The game ends when each pair has had a go at being 'connected'.

Game: Word tennis
Difficulty rating: **
Minimum number of participants: 2
Resources needed: Clear space
Instructions: This activity can be done in pairs, small groups or one large group. The leader gives each pair/ group a topic, and they have to say words connected with it. They are out if they say a word that is not connected to the topic or if they pause for more than five seconds.

Suggested topics:

- girls' names
- boys' names
- fruit
- sports
- colours
- animals
- occupations
- countries
- transport
- birds
- pets
- sweets
- chocolate bars
- TV shows
- superheroes
- fairy tales
- cartoons
- films

Game: 20 questions
Difficulty rating: ***
Minimum number of participants: 3
Resources needed: Clear space
Instructions: One child sits in the middle of a circle of children and thinks of an animal or person. The rest of the class must ask questions to try to guess the animal or person. The child in the centre can reply only "yes" or "no". If no one has guessed correctly after 20 questions have been asked, the child in the centre thinks of another animal or person. When someone guesses correctly, s/he goes into the centre of the circle and thinks of a different animal or person. The game continues until everyone has had a chance to be in the centre.

Game: Just 30 seconds
Difficulty rating: ****
Minimum number of participants: 3
Resources needed: Stopwatch (or watch with a second hand), list of topics
Instructions: Each child is given a topic. They have 30 seconds to gather their thoughts and then they must speak for 30 seconds on it. If s/he thinks it's appropriate, the leader can introduce a few rules, such as no speech interjections like "umm" or "ahh" or no deliberately long pauses.

The following are some of the topics that can be used:
- o boys
- o girls
- o school
- o sports
- o chocolate
- o leaders
- o friends
- o TV
- o books
- o football
- o family
- o clothes
- o mobile phones
- o computers
- o internet
- o texting
- o flowers
- o winter
- o holidays
- o summer

Concentration Games

The following concentration activities help children with their observation skills. One of the benefits of these games is that they can be played in a restricted space.

They help children to develop a sustained focus of the mind, body and voice, which also helps with general school life.

Game: Clap and tap
Difficulty rating: **
Minimum number of participants: 4
Resources needed: Clear space
Instructions: The children sit in a circle. The leader claps twice and taps a part of her/his body with both hands. For example, clap, clap, tap head; clap, clap, tap knees, and so on. The children follow what the leader does. It becomes more complicated and faster as the children get used to following the leader. If a child makes a mistake, s/he is out. The last one in can be the leader the next time.

Variation: The leader instructs the children that one clap means stand, two claps mean stand on one leg and three claps mean sit. The leader or one of the members of the group stands in the centre and claps instructions. The children must listen very carefully to the clapped instructions. If they fail to do the correct action, they are out.

Game: Tell it
Difficulty rating: ****
Minimum number of participants: 2
Resources needed: Clear space
Instructions: Divide the group into pairs. Both children must begin to tell a story at the same time. The object of this game is to see if the children can listen and talk at once. After a few minutes, the leader will shout "stop," and each child tells the other child what they heard.

Game: Mirrors
Difficulty rating: ***
Minimum number of participants: 2
Resources needed: Clear space
Instructions: Divide the group into pairs: one child is A and the other is B. They must stand opposite each other. The leader explains that A is going to be the mirror and B is going to be looking into the mirror. B starts to do actions very slowly, and A has to copy what B does. The actions can get faster and faster. After a few minutes, they swap roles.

Game: 20-to-1
Difficulty rating: ****
Minimum number of participants: 10
Resources needed: Clear space
Instructions: This is a fun game that leads to a lot of hilarity and is more difficult than it first seems. Everyone stands in a circle. The objective of the game is for the group to count from 1 to 20, but the difficulty is that no one is assigned to say the next number. The leader starts by saying one and anyone else in the group can say two. But if two children say a number at the same time, the game has to start again at number one. The leader may have to impose some rules, such as the children can't just go around the circle and count in order. This is a good concentration game and it is also very good for building teamwork.

Game: Follow the leader
Difficulty rating: *
Minimum number of participants: 5
Resources needed: Clear space
Instructions: Everyone sits in a circle and one child volunteers to leave the room. While the volunteer is outside, someone is chosen to be the leader. Before the volunteer comes back, the leader starts to do an action and the others imitate her/him. When the volunteer returns, s/he has to guess the identity of the leader.

The leader can change the action when the volunteer isn't looking. The volunteer can guess three times. When s/he has guessed correctly or has been told who the leader is after the third incorrect guess, someone else volunteers to leave the room, a new leader is chosen and the game continues.

Game: Emotions
Difficulty rating: ****
Minimum number of participants: 3
Resources needed: Clear space, index cards with a different emotion written on each one
Instructions: The leader explains to the children that s/he is going to call out an emotion and they must show that emotion on their faces for 20 seconds.

Some sample emotions:
- o bored
- o confused
- o happy

o hurt
o amused
o forgetful
o angry
o delighted
o desperate
o upset
o relieved

Everyone in the class must try to maintain each expression for 20 seconds, even if other children lose it! If children cannot sustain it for 20 seconds, they are out.

For a greater challenge, tell the children to try to transition between the scenarios and emotions below convincingly!

Try out the following:
o waiting for something
o confusion
o physical ache or pain
o thinking about something deeply
o bored
o something caught my attention
o quietly amused
o trying to remember something, but failing
o remembering something painful
o remembering something happy
o frustration
o anger
o elation
o trying to hide your irritation
o scheming or devising a plan
o despair
o verge of tears
o relief

Now let's try some more complex techniques, still involving no words:
o guffaw (short laugh)
o sniff – perhaps to show awkwardness
o clearing throat – perhaps to show you're trying to clear your thoughts or perhaps to get someone's attention
o sigh – perhaps from tiredness or perhaps because you're relieved or frustrated
o muttering in panic, irritation or disbelief
o mmmm – perhaps thinking or 'agreeing with yourself' or confirming your own thoughts

Game: Change it
Difficulty rating: ***
Minimum number of participants: 4
Resources needed: Clear space
Instructions: This game requires a lot of attention and concentration. A leader is chosen and makes a movement. The leader calls out "change" and changes his/her movement. The others in the group must then do the leader's previous movement.

Example:
- o Leader claps hands; rest of group stands still.
- o Leader shouts "change," and bends knees; rest of the group claps hands.
- o Leader shouts "change," and stomps feet; rest of the group bends knees.

If anyone makes a mistake or does the wrong action, they are out. The leader can shout "change" as many times and as quickly as s/he wants.

Game: Wink murder
Difficulty rating: ***
Minimum number of participants: 6
Resources needed: Clear space, blank pieces of paper, one piece of paper with 'D' on it and one with 'M' on it.
Instructions: The leader hands out pieces of paper, one of which has a D on it which means that child is the detective, and one of which has a M on it, which means that child is the murderer. The rest of the sheets are blank.

The detective makes himself known to everyone; the murderer remains anonymous. The leader explains that the murderer kills people by winking at them. When the children are winked at, they must 'die' dramatically. The children sit in a circle around the detective, whose objective is to correctly identify the murderer before s/he commits a murder. A limit should be imposed upon the number of accusations the detective can make, for example if the murderer manages to kill three victims before the detective identifies them, s/he wins the game.

Game: Pass the face
Difficulty rating: ***
Minimum number of participants: 3
Resources needed: Clear space
Instructions: Everyone stands in a circle. A child is selected and has to make a face, expressing a feeling or emotion. S/He doesn't tell anyone what the feeling is but shows 'the face' to the child next to him/her in the circle. Then that child passes on 'the face' to the next child in the circle. The last child in the circle must guess what emotion the first child was trying to convey.

Game: Swaps
Difficulty rating: ***
Minimum number of participants: 3
Resources needed: Clear space
Instructions: One child volunteers to leave the room. When s/he has left, the rest of the group change some items of their clothing like jewellery, shoes, jumpers and so on. When the volunteer comes back, s/he has to guess what was changed. You can specify the number of changes the children can make or you can let them decide themselves....

Storytelling Games

Storytelling games are very important in any learning environment. They are particularly important when working with children as they encourage them to use their imaginations. The games also help to instil confidence in children and to develop both their receptive and expressive skills.

The following activities are a fun and enjoyable way of developing storytelling techniques.

Game: One-word story
Difficulty rating: ***
Minimum number of participants: 5
Resources needed: Clear space
Instructions: The children sit in a circle, and the leader tells them to create a story as a group. One child volunteers to start the story and says a word. The next child in the circle adds a second word to the story, and the next child does the same, until everyone in the circle has contributed one word. The story goes around the circle a few times. It is important that the story makes grammatical sense.

Variation: You can do the same activity using whole sentences instead of single words.

Game: Unfortunately/fortunately
Difficulty rating: *****
Minimum number of participants: 3
Resources needed: Clear space
Instructions: This is an extension of the one-word/one-sentence story. The children sit in a circle. The leader begins the story; then each child in turn contributes one sentence to the story. This time, however, they must alternately say "fortunately" or "unfortunately" before each sentence.

Example:
Leader: One day there was a pilot flying a plane.
Child 1: Fortunately he had a tank full of petrol.
Child 2: Unfortunately the engine failed.
Child 3: Fortunately he had a parachute so he jumped out of the plane.
Child 4: Unfortunately the parachute wouldn't open.
Child 5: Fortunately he fell on top of a haystack.
Child 6: Unfortunately in the haystack there was a pitchfork.
And so on.

Game: First-liners/last-liners
Difficulty rating: ***
Minimum number of participants: 4
Resources needed: Clear space
Instructions: Divide the class into groups of three or four. Give each group a line and the children must come up with a story that starts with that line.

Examples:
- o It was a dark and stormy night.
- o "Wake up! Wake up!" she screamed.
- o "Oh look what has happened," she sighed. "I told you not to eat it."
- o "I wouldn't go into that room if I were you," she said.

An extension of this activity is that each group gets a sentence that the story must finish with:
- o And then he ate the goldfish.
- o "Quick, run!"
- o "I was only joking," he said.
- o She couldn't believe how much money she owed.

It is important to give the children 10 or 15 minutes to come up with their stories. Each group then has to narrate its story, with every child contributing.

Game: Three lies and a truth
Difficulty rating: *
Minimum number of participants: 3
Resources needed: Pens and paper
Instructions: Give each child a piece of paper and a pen. Have them divide their sheet of paper into four sections. In three of the sections, they must write down lies, and in the fourth, they must write down a truth. The rest of the class must guess which statements are lies and which one is the truth.

The lies/truth can be very simple or very elaborate. It is up to each child to decide. Encourage them to use their imaginations.

Game: An embarrassing moment
Difficulty rating: ***
Minimum number of participants: 8
Resources needed: Clear space
Instructions: This is a very enjoyable game that children find fun. Divide the class into groups of four. Each group discusses embarrassing situations. The first group chooses one embarrassing situation, and all the children tell the other groups the story. The rest of the groups must guess which child originally told the story.

Game: No "s" sounds game
Difficulty rating: ****
Minimum number of participants: 3
Resources needed: Clear Space
Instructions: A child tells a story but without using or saying the letter "s". The story gets faster and faster, until a child makes a mistake. When s/he makes a mistake, they are out.

　　　As an alternative, the leader can change the forbidden letter from "s" to e.g. "t".

Game: Mixed-up fairy tales
Difficulty rating: ****
Minimum number of participants: 6
Resources needed: Index cards with names of fairy tales
Instructions: Discuss different types of fairy tales. Then divide the class into groups of three or four and have each group choose a card. Give them five minutes to prepare their fairy tale, but each group must perform it for the other groups in less than one minute.

Fairy tale suggestions:
- *Little Red Riding Hood*
- *Sleeping Beauty*
- *Rapunzel*
- *Beauty and the Beast*
- *Hansel and Gretel*
- *Snow White and the Seven Dwarfs*
- *The Ugly Duckling*
- *Puss in Boots*

Game: Pop-up story book
Difficulty rating: *
Minimum number of participants: 3
Resources needed: Clear space, story book
Instructions: This is also an excellent listening game that can be played with any number of children. The teacher chooses a story to read that the children are familiar with. Each child is given a word from the story. For example, if the teacher was reading 'Goldilocks and the Three Bears:' one child may be given the word Goldilocks; another child has the word baby; another, porridge; another, bed, and so on. When each child has been given a word, the game begins. All the children lie on the floor, and when a child hears their word, s/he jumps up. If a child misses their word, s/he is out and can't pop up anymore.

Game: Fill in the gaps
Difficulty rating: **
Minimum number of participants: 3
Resources needed: Handouts with the story on it
Instructions: Give each child or group of three children a copy of the following story and have them fill in the gaps. They then have to read their story out to the rest of the class.

Once upon a time, there was a _____ Prince. He lived in a very _____ castle with _____ and _____. Near the castle there was a _____ forest.

One day he was _____ and he decided to go into the forest. He walked farther and farther into the forest and then he felt _____. Suddenly he saw _____ and he _____. He met a _____ who told him that _____.

The prince was very _____ and he wanted to _____. It was getting late so he turned back toward the castle. He was _____ and felt _____.

Finally he arrived home. He was _____.
He woke up the next day and he _____. He met _____ and told him _____. The Prince was _____ to be home.

Improvisation Games

These are the most difficult activities in the book. Improvisation develops skills such as confidence and empathy.

These activities give children an outlet to express a range of emotions.

Game: Three words
Difficulty rating: ****
Minimum number of participants: 3
Resources needed: Clear space
Instructions: Divide the class into small groups of three or four and give each group three words: hello, sorry and why. Tell each group they have five minutes to come up with a scene that tells a story, but they can speak only these three words. Each group then performs the scene for the rest of the class.

When they have all performed, give each group another five minutes to practice the same sketch, but this time they can use as much dialogue as they want.

Game: Headlines
Difficulty rating: ***
Minimum number of participants: 4
Resources needed: News headlines and pictures
Instructions: Divide the class into groups of four or five. Give each group a headline from a newspaper. They can be fun headlines or news of a more serious nature. Each group gets five minutes, with five still images that tell the story of that headline. The leader gets the images from various newspapers. Each group then shows these images to the rest of the class, who must guess each headline.

The students then return to their groups and create an improvisation of the news headline, with actions and speech.

Game: Magical fairy tales
Difficulty rating: ***
Minimum number of participants: 4
Resources needed: Three lists – one with characters; one with settings; and one with objects.
Instructions: Create three lists with the suggestions below or come up with your own ideas. On the first list you need a variety of characters, for example:

- o Cinderella
- o The Troll (from *Three Billy Goats' Gruff*)
- o Snow White
- o The Wicked Queen
- o The Bad Fairy (from *Sleeping Beauty*)
- o Gingerbread Man
- o The Wicked Wolf

○ Little Bo Peep
○ Pinocchio
○ Jack (from *Jack and Jill*)
○ Jill
○ The Beast (from *Beauty and the Beast*)
○ Little Miss Muffet
○ One of the Three Little Pigs
○ Prince Charming
○ Jack (from *Jack and the Beanstalk*)
○ Ugly Duckling
○ Fairy Godmother

The second list is a variety of places. Here are some suggestions:
○ a castle
○ a dragon's cave
○ a haunted house
○ a jail cell
○ a superhero's house
○ a dark forest
○ a stolen ship
○ a wolf's den
○ a dungeon

The final list is a variety of magical objects. Here are some suggestions:
○ magic wand
○ magic beans
○ magic kisses
○ a genie
○ magical dust
○ magic ring
○ magic potions
○ magic carpets
○ magic lamps
○ magic swords
○ cloak of invisibility

Divide the students into groups of three of four and have each child choose a character. When they have chosen their characters, each group must choose one setting and one magical item. They can pick these randomly out of a hat or can choose from the list, whichever the leader prefers. In their groups, the children make up a story, using their chosen characters, setting and magical object.

If they are more advanced, they can do an improvisation based on what they have chosen.

Game: Dilemmas
Difficulty rating: *****
Minimum number of participants: 6
Resources needed: Clear space, index cards with different dilemmas with possible resolutions written on them.
Instructions: The children choose a dilemma card and in groups they devise a short scene which shows someone in a dilemma. They perform the dilemma for the other children. The leader freezes the drama at a point of dramatic tension, for example when the character is faced with the dilemma. The audience has to try to guess the outcome. The group then performs the ending to show the audience if it was right. Then the group rewinds the scene and shows an alternative ending.

Variations: show all in one go – starting with freezing at the moment of tension and then running the full scene to show the bad ending and rewinding to show the positive ending.

Game: Hitchhiker
Difficulty rating: ****
Minimum number of participants: 4
Resources needed: Index cards, 4 chairs.
Instructions: Place four chairs so that two are in front and two behind, like the inside of a car. One child volunteers to be the driver. The driver picks up three hitchhikers one at a time. Each hitchhiker has a hidden agenda and the rest of the group has to guess it.

Some examples for the hitchhiker game – the hitchhiker is:
- o obsessed with colours or a certain colour e.g. red, yellow
- o obsessed with numbers or a certain number e.g. 3.7
- o is in love with him/herself
- o can't say words with the letter S in them
- o thinks they are a fairytale character – the leader/child can choose character
- o thinks they are a TV character – the leader/child can choose
- o loves football or any other sport

Game: Nursery rhyme news
Difficulty rating: ***
Minimum number of participants: 5
Resources needed: Nursery rhymes
Instructions: Divide the class into groups of five. Each group chooses a nursery rhyme from the list below. In their groups, they must come up with a news story relating to the nursery rhyme. They can have a newscaster and a journalist reporting live from the scene, interviewing witnesses about what's happened. They could speak to a character in the nursery rhyme.

For example: Humpty Dumpty.
The improvisation could start with the newscaster who announces some breaking news: "It has just been reported that the giant egg *Humpty Dumpty* has fallen off his wall. Reports from the scene are that the king's horses and men are trying to help with this disaster. Now we are going live to our reporter ...... who is on scene." Then the reporter explains what is happening.

The following nursery rhymes can be used:

Twinkle, twinkle, little star
Twinkle, twinkle, little star,
How I wonder what you are.
Up above the world so high,
Like a diamond in the sky.
Twinkle, twinkle, little star,
How I wonder what you are!

Mary had a little lamb
Mary had a little lamb,
Little lamb, little lamb,
Mary had a little lamb,
Whose fleece was white as snow.
And everywhere that Mary went,
Mary went, Mary went,
And everywhere that Mary went,
The lamb was sure to go.
It followed her to school one day
School one day, school one day,
It followed her to school one day,
Which was against the rules.
It made the children laugh and play,
Laugh and play, laugh and play,
It made the children laugh and play
To see a lamb at school.

The itsy bitsy spider
The itsy bitsy spider crawled up the water spout.
Down came the rain, and washed the spider out.
Out came the sun, and dried up all the rain,
And the itsy bitsy spider went up the spout again.

Hickory Dickory Dock
Hickory Dickory Dock,
The mouse ran up the clock.
The clock struck one,
The mouse ran down!
Hickory Dickory Dock.

Little Bo Peep
Little Bo-peep has lost her sheep,
And doesn't know where to find them.
Leave them alone and they'll come home,
Wagging their tails behind them.
Little Bo-peep fell fast asleep,
And dreamt she heard them bleating;
But when she awoke, she found it a joke,
For they were still a-fleeting.
Then up she took her little crook,
Determined for to find them;
She found them indeed, but it made her heart bleed,
For they'd left all their tails behind them.

Jack and Jill
Jack and Jill went up the hill
To fetch a pail of water.
Jack fell down and broke his crown
And Jill came tumbling after.

Game: Death in a minute
Difficulty rating: ****
Minimum number of participants: 8
Resources needed: Clear space
Instructions: Divide the class into groups of four or five. Give each group a few minutes to improvise a one-minute sketch in which someone dies at the end. The improvisation can be mad, sad or funny. Each group performs for the others.

The leader keeps time and tells them when they have 10 seconds left. The children must stick to the time limit, and the improvisation has to make sense. At the end the whole class can discuss how effectively each group kept to the rules.

Game: Create a moving picture
Difficulty rating: **
Minimum number of participants: 4
Resources needed: Clear space
Instructions: Define a space and have the group stand outside the area. The group are numbered from one upwards. Number 1 runs into the designated space and shouts for example: "I'm a tree," and then she freezes as a tree. Number 2 runs into the designated space and says: "I'm a park bench." Number 3: "I'm a child sitting on the bench." Number 4: "I'm a swing." Number 5: "I'm a child swinging on the swing," and so on until every child has a part in the picture. When everyone has a role, the picture comes to life and starts moving. If they wish, the students can start making noise and talking.

Game: Emotional chairs
Difficulty rating: ***
Minimum number of participants: 4
Resources needed: Clear space, chairs
Instructions: The leader puts two chairs beside each other. Two children volunteer to sit on the chairs, and the leader whispers an emotion to each child. Each student must act out the emotion using only body language. Then the leader tells them to start a dialogue and the pair has a conversation, starting with a greeting. They must portray their assigned emotions throughout the dialogue. The rest of the class must try to guess the emotions. The two children who guess correctly are the next ones to sit in the chairs.

Ideas for emotions:
- o excited
- o upset
- o happy
- o sad
- o angry
- o passionate
- o surprised
- o frightened
- o nervous

Game: Pick and mix
Difficulty rating: ***
Minimum number of participants: 4
Resources needed: Eighteen index cards – six with animals, six with objects and six with fairy-tale characters.
Instructions: This is a fun improvisation that children always enjoy. The leader makes three stacks of the different cards. Divide the class into groups of four or five. Each group picks a card from each stack. Based on the cards they have chosen, they create an improvisation. For example: The Elephant, the Princess and the Key.

Ideas for wild animals:
- o elephant
- o tiger
- o hippopotamus
- o crocodile
- o monkey
- o hyena
- o giraffe
- o gazelle
- o zebra
- o rhinoceros

Ideas for fairy-tale characters:
- o a princess
- o a prince
- o a witch
- o a huntsman
- o a dwarf
- o an ugly stepsister
- o a woodcutter
- o a king/queen
- o genie
- o gingerbread man

Ideas for objects:
- o key
- o chair
- o castle
- o cave
- o cup
- o pen
- o tree
- o ring
- o blanket
- o phone

Part Two: Plays for Children

The following five plays are suitable for children age nine and older. The suggestions for stage directions are included in brackets and italics. The cast list is flexible – more characters can be added and existing characters can be changed or omitted. The costumes are very simple; the children can wear something in the colour of their animal, wear a mask or use some face paint. If the children wear a mask, make sure it isn't covering their mouths as it would make it difficult to hear them when they speak.

Each play lasts between 10 and 15 minutes.

How the Zebra Got His Stripes

Cast of Characters (20): 2 Narrators – can be jungle animals; 1 Zebra; 1 Eagle; 1 Elephant; 2 Giraffes; 1 Lion; 1 Leopard; 2 Gazelles; 2 Ostriches; 1 Peacock; 3 Monkeys; 2 Hyenas; 1 Rhinoceros.

(Stage Directions: Curtains open on all the animals in the jungle. They dance to animal-style music something like The Circle of Life *or music from* The Jungle Book.)

Narrator 1: Long ago, in the hot, dry grasslands of Africa's great Savannah, all of the animals lived, but they all had dull coats and looked the same. None of them looked distinctive.

(All the animals milling around the stage look the same, but their walks and body language makes them different.)

Narrator 2: They would work together to collect food to last throughout the summer's drought.

Narrator 1: The only animals that didn't pull their weight in the Savannah were the lazy lion, the foolish rhinoceros and the extremely greedy zebra. These animals would sit around eating all day, their knobbly legs protruding from under their fat stomachs.

(Zebra, Rhino and Lion are sitting on the left side of stage, eating.)

Narrator 2: The elephant, who was the noblest and wisest animal in all the animal kingdom, would sometimes scold Zebra and his friends. Leopard went with him.

(Elephant walks towards Zebra, Rhino and Lion.)

Elephant: Zebra, don't you think you should help everyone else? We all must collect food and water so we will not starve in the hot summer.

Leopard: Yes, you know how hot it gets. Everything dies. We must make sure we have enough food to survive.

Lion: Oh, go away Elephant and Leopard; we are hungry now.

Zebra: We want to eat what we want now. *(Points to a tree.)* Come on, Rhino, look, lovely lush green trees over there.

Rhino: Quick, hurry before those goody-two-shoes try to save some of it for the summer drought.

(Zebra and Rhino are laughing and joking and eating the leaves on the tree, while Lion sits in shade eating a big slab of meat.)

Giraffe 1: *(Puts his arm around Elephant.)* Do not take any notice of them Elephant. They are not very nice animals. Rhino is foolish; Lion is lazy and Zebra is just … well, Zebra is just plain … grrrrrrrrrrrrrreeeeeedy:

Leopard: Come on Elephant and Giraffe, we don't need them. We can ask the other animals to help us.

(Eagle comes swooping on to the stage.)

Eagle: Why do you look so glum Elephant?

Giraffe 2: Hello, Eagle. We have asked Lion, Zebra and Rhino to help us to collect food for the winter, but they just want to stuff their faces now and not save any food.

Leopard: While we do all the work!

Eagle: Don't take any notice of them. I will help you because I can fly up into the sky and survey the hot plains and find the best food. Then we can all work together and get the food for the long, hot summer.

Elephant: What a splendid idea, Eagle. Giraffe, call the ostriches. Leopard, get the gazelles and I will get Peacock.

(Monkeys arrive on stage, swinging from the trees)

Monkeys: What about us? We want to help to collect the food.

Giraffe 1: Mmmmmmmmm. Monkeys, you don't know how to behave yourselves. You can only help if you promise to do it properly.

Eagle: Yes, Monkeys, you can't be getting into mischief like you normally do.

Monkey 1: We promise.

Monkey 2: Oh, please, let us come.

Elephant: I don't know. Your mischief will delay us.

(Flashbacks to the tricks the monkeys played on the other animals in the jungle. For example, they could run away, knock on the ostriches as their heads are in the sand or scare the gazelles by pretending to be monsters. Ask for suggestions from the students. Let them come up with their own ideas. Act out the flashbacks. Make them as funny as you can.)

Peacock: I haven't forgiven you, you know.

Ostriches: *(very angry)* Neither have we.

Elephant: Perhaps they deserve a second chance.

Gazelle 1: Well, leopards never change their spots.

Gazelle 2: *(Very meekly looks at Leopard who looks annoyed.)* No offence meant, Leopard.

Leopard: *(Looks annoyed)* None taken. But I don't know why everybody says that because I don't have any spots.

Narrator 2: All the animals worked hard except for Lion, Rhino and Zebra.

(Lion, Zebra and Rhino are sunning themselves, eating, chatting, and playing.)

(The animals mime working hard while Lion, Rhino and Zebra are sleeping, playing and eating. Music could be played while the animals are moving.)

Narrator 1: One stormy day in the heart of the African plains there was a rumbling in the Earth. *(Thunder sounds and the lights flick on and off.)*

Narrator 2: Then all of a sudden a huge cave appeared in the ground.

Giraffe: What was all that noise?

Gazelle 1: I don't know, but it was very scary.

Gazelle 2: *(Both the gazelles are in a huddle.)* Look over there.

Hyenas: *(Laughing nervously)* Everyone needs to be careful.

Ostrich 1: I am not staying here.

Ostrich 2: Me neither. *(They bury their heads.)*

Narrator 1: A few animals crept cautiously up to this new and wonderful sight, and when Leopard, who was the bravest of them all, peered into the darkness, he saw something glittering.

Leopard: There is a big hole and there is something glittering inside it.

Monkeys: Come quickly, let's have a look.

Peacock: No, we have to be careful. We must wait for Elephant to see if he knows anything about this wonderful sight. Besides, I don't want to get myself dirty.

Narrator 1: Just then they heard the thunderous plodding of the elephant.

Leopard: Elephant come and have look at this. What do you think it is?

Elephant: I'm not sure, but I will go ask my friend Eagle. Eagle knows all the secrets of the African Plains. You stay here. Don't move a muscle, and I will try to find Eagle.

(All the animals freeze or the curtain closes.)

(Elephant and Eagle appear on-stage, entering from either side, and stand in front of the curtain.)

Elephant: Eagle, what is going on here? Do you know what is happening?

(Eagle whispers something into Elephant's ear.)

(Eagle leaves and Elephant calls the other animals.)

Elephant: Leopard! Giraffe! Ostriches! Peacock! Monkeys! Hyenas! Come quickly everyone. Gazelles! Zebra! Lion! Rhino!

(The animals come in from the back of the auditorium, except for Zebra, Lion and Rhino. The rest of the animals greet the audience, waving and smiling at them.)

Peacock: Well Elephant, what is the story?

Elephant: There are all kinds of materials in the cave which you may choose from. You will be issued needles by the Ostriches so that you can sew your beautiful new coats, but there is only one needle each so take good care of it.

Ostrich 1: Roll up, roll up, get your needles here.

Ostrich 2: Only one for each animal. Lose them at your peril.

(All the animals line-up and receive their needles.)

Elephant: Now you may go in, but there is to be no pushing and shoving. Keep in an orderly line.

Gazelles: Everyone is here except for Lion, Rhino and greedy Zebra.

Peacock: They don't want to come. They are too busy munching on the grass and playing. If they don't come, there will be more for us.

Elephant: Let them be. Come, hurry up. You are going to miss out.

(While the curtain is closed the stage hands create an illusion of a cave by spreading different types of material and props such as horns for the Rhino. The animals all go into the cave as the curtains open.)

Narrator 1: The animals were amazed. The cave was full of furs and skins, all glossy and new.

(All the animals are in the cave except for Rhino, Lion and Zebra, who are now grazing stage right.)

Narrator 2: Inside the cave, there were horns and tails of countless shapes and sizes, and lots of threads of a thousand different colours.

Narrator 1: The news spread far and wide and soon all the animals were on their way to see the cave, running and jumping, sliding and swinging, and slithering through the trees.

(The animals enter the cave one-by-one, every few seconds – the Monkeys, Hyenas and so on. Eventually Lion arrives at the cave, and he is followed by Rhino, who looks on rather sheepishly.)

Elephant: Where is greedy Zebra?

Rhino: He didn't want to come. He said there was lots of time to go visiting the cave.

Lion: He is too busy stuffing grass into his bulging mouth.

Hyenas: *(laugh)*

(The Monkeys jump around, doing impressions of a fat zebra.)

(Music plays and all the animals admire themselves and help put things on each other. Everyone focuses on Peacock.)

(Music fades out and curtain closes and Zebra is lying on the stage steps, half asleep and munching grass.)

Zebra: All those silly animals are gone to see the cave. I don't care as there is more food for me. Yummy, yummy!

(One-by-one the animals come out from behind the curtains. Zebra becomes more and more amazed as the animals get more and more spectacular until it culminates in Peacock or whoever has the most colourful costume. It is like a catwalk in a fashion show. The narrators can describe what everyone is wearing, as the animals walk up the centre of the theatre and back down and pose for a few seconds. They walk back up on the stage and behind the curtains which are still closed.)

(Zebra is amazed by all this, and when the fashion show is finished, he talks to the audience.)

Zebra: I am going to be the most beautiful animal in the jungle. I shall have spots like Leopard, beautiful feathers like Peacock and a gorgeous mane like Lion. I will be the finest looking animal in Africa.

(Asks the audience which animal they prefer and what sort of things they would like to see him wear.)

(Curtains open and only Rhino and Elephant are on the stage.)

Elephant: Rhino, there is only grey left because it took you so long to choose. But here have a horn.

(Rhino puts on the horn but puts it on wrong.)

Rhino: I put the horn on wrong.

Elephant: I will help you to straighten it. *(Struggles to help him)* No, there is nothing I can do.

Rhino: I suppose I will have to live with the horn.

Elephant: Oh, stop complaining. At least you have a horn; I am just left the grey material.

Zebra: *(Climbs onto the stage.)* I have come to deck myself out in wonderful colours and furs.

Elephant: There is nothing left.

Rhino: I got the last of the horns.

Elephant: There may be a few bits of black material over there, but to be honest, I think you are too late.

(Elephant and Rhino leave the stage.)

Narrator 1: Zebra searched desperately and found some black material.

Zebra: It is a bit tight, but I can squeeze in to it. What do you think? *(Asks the audience what they think.)*

Narrator 2: Zebra pushed and grunted, oohed and aahed and finally he managed to squeeze himself into the black cloth.

Narrator 1: But it was a tight fit. It was bursting at the seams, especially around his fat tummy.

Zebra: I feel a bit peckish. I think I will stroll down to the stream to take a quick bite of a leafy bush.

Narrator 2: When suddenly pop, pop, pop. His tubby tummy squeezed through the seams.

(All the animals come in and laugh at him.)

Eagle: To this day his chubby stomach shines through his coat because he is so …

GRRRRRRRRRRRRRRREEEEEEEEEEEEEEEEDDDDDDDDDY!

The Selfish Giant

Cast of Characters (23): The Selfish Giant; The Cornish Ogre; 3 parts of the wall – Sad, Lazy and Frightened; 2 Trees; Ice; Frost; Snow; Wind; Narrator/Old man; 8 Children – Anna/Billy/Cathy/Ger/Dick/Ellie/Fred/Harry; 2 grandchildren.

(Stage Directions: curtains are closed. The opening scene is an old man sitting with his two grandchildren grouped around him, sitting downstage left. Selfish Giant and Cornish Ogre are sitting centre stage, miming drinking tea and talking.)

Narrator/Old man: Children come over here and I will tell you the story of a giant that lived a long time ago. He had a lovely, beautiful garden with soft, green grass. There were the most amazing flowers and 12 fabulous peach trees. However, the giant was very selfish, and he shared his garden with no one.

Old Man: He used to say...

Selfish Giant: My own garden is my own garden and no one else can use it!

Old Man: The giant had been to visit his friend the Cornish Ogre and stayed seven years.

(Giant and Ogre drink tea and mime having a conversation.)

Selfish Giant: I have been here for seven years, and we have run out of things to talk about.

Cornish Ogre: Yes, you have been here a long time, so maybe it is time you went back to your beautiful, empty garden.

Old Man: They said goodbye and the Selfish Giant returned home.

(Giant waves goodbye and they both leave the stage, going in different directions.)

However, what the Selfish Giant didn't know was that his garden was being used by the local school children.

(School bell rings. Eight children run up the centre aisle and start to play with the children in the audience. They run down the side aisles and reach the steps to the stage. The curtains open and there is a wall centre stage, with three parts to it: there is the happy part of the wall; a frightened part of the wall; and a lazy part of the wall. The lazy part is in the centre. There are also two trees on each side of the stage: centre stage left and centre stage right. The children squeeze through a hole in the wall.)

Anna: Right, I've got through! Come on, Cathy. I'll give you a hand. Mind the nettles.

Billy: Ouch! Take care, Cathy, the nettles are very bad today. Watch out.

Cathy: All right. Nearly through. *(She pushes her way in.)* That's it. Here at last. *(Sighing)* Wonderful!

(Children chat as four more go through the hole, one-by-one.)

Dick: *(The last one trying to get through and having difficulty.)* This hole seems to be getting smaller and smaller, unless it's my imagination.

Ellie: No, you've got that wrong Dick. You're getting fatter. It's all that fast food you eat.

(Children all laugh and pull Dick through the hole!)

Ger: I love this place so much, and I am so happy when we are all in here playing.

(Everyone agrees by nodding their heads.)

Harry: It's seven years since the giant was here. I know it's his garden, but he can't come back after all this time, can he?

Fred: I hope not. But just in case we'd better make the most of it while we've got it.

(Children go off-stage. Lights focus on the three parts of the wall.)

Frightened: Wake up, Lazy. If the Selfish Giant comes back, we will be in trouble.

Lazy: The giant hasn't been here for seven years. I am tired of holding up the centre of the wall.

Happy: I love seeing all the children playing in the garden. I am so happy when they come into the garden, but, Lazy, I think you should wake-up.

Lazy: I am going back to sleep. *(Starts snoring.)*

Frightened: I'm scared. I have a bad feeling.

Happy: You are always scared. Try to cheer up and be happy that the sun is shining and the children are having such a good time playing in the garden.

Tree 1: Lazy needs to wake-up.

Tree 2: Why don't we ask the audience to help us?

Tree 1: That's a good idea. When we count to three, everyone must say, "Wake-up, Lazy."

Happy, Frightened and the trees: One, two, three audience, everybody together – wake-up, Lazy.

(Eight Children come back on the stage and the trees and the two parts of the wall freeze.)

Fred: Let's play a game of stuck in the mud!

Ger: No, that's really boring.

Ellie: I know! Let's play Giant's footsteps.

Billy: That's not funny.

Dick: What about blind man's bluff?

All: Oh yes!

Cathy: Here's my tie. Come on, Fred. Ready for the blindfold?

Fred: I'm not doing it.

Anna: You are a scaredy-cat.

All except Fred and Harry: Scaredy-cat; scaredy-cat.

Harry: Leave him alone, I will do it.

(Harry is blindfolded and the game begins. They run around having fun. There is the sound of footsteps.)

Tree 1: Did you hear that?

Tree 2: Hear what?

Frightened: I hear it too. Wake up, Lazy.

Lazy: I'm sleeping.

(Giant enters while the children are playing.)

Happy: Lazy, I think you need to wake up. NOW!

(All the children see the giant and they begin to squirm and then all run away.)

Giant: How earth did those horrible children get inside my garden.

(Looks at the wall and sees Lazy only half-standing up.)

Giant: I see where the problem is. Lazy, wake-up now!

(Lazy jumps up and stands at attention.)

Frightened: *(whispers)* I told you he was going to come back.

Giant: Wall, if you don't stand up properly, I am going to knock you down and build a new, stronger wall. This is my garden and NO ONE is allowed in here. I know what I'm going to do. I'm going to put up a sign.

(Giant gets a sign and puts it around Lazy's neck.)

Giant: *(Shouts at the children.)* Can you read this sign, you horrible children?

Children: Trespassers will be presecutED.

Giant: No, you ignorant children. It is TRESPASSERS will be PROSECUTED.

Lazy: What does that mean?

Happy: It means anyone will be in trouble if they come into the garden.

(Giant exits muttering. Curtains close to change the scene.)

Narrator/Old Man: Now the children had nowhere to play.

(Curtains open: the stage has changed, as the trees are now behind the wall and they are all upstage to give the illusion that the children are outside the garden.)

Anna: Why does the giant have to be so mean?

Billy: We have nowhere to play now.

Cathy: We weren't doing him any harm.

Dick: Where will we play now?

Ellie: The road!

Fred: We could get knocked down.

Ger: We have no choice now.

(The children look forlorn and play with their heads down.)

(They all look toward the garden.)

Harry: How happy we were there!

(The children slowly walk off the stage.)

Narrator/Old Man: Then spring came over the country. There were flowers blooming, trees in blossom and birds singing. Only in the garden of the selfish giant it was still winter. The birds did not care to sing in it as there were no children. And the flowers had no heart to bloom.

Ice: Well Frost, I think our work has been done here.

Frost: I'm looking forward to having a break.

(Ice suddenly notices the sign: 'Trespassers will be prosecuted.')

Ice: Look at this.

Frost: That Selfish Giant won't share his garden.

Ice: I know. Let's stay here until the Selfish Giant learns to share his beautiful garden.

Frost: I know, I will call Wind and Snow and get them to come and help. *(Takes out mobile phone and rings them. Wind shows up immediately.)*

Wind: What's the big emergency? I was very busy in Florida. It is hurricane season, you know.

Ice: Wait until Snow gets here and we will tell you all about it.

(A few seconds late Snow arrives on-stage.)

Snow: I'm here.

Wind: What took you so long?

Snow: I was in Lapland helping Santa. What's the big emergency?

Frost: Anyway, look at this sign. The Selfish Giant won't share his garden, so we are going to stay here until he changes his mind.

(Ice, Frost, Wind and Snow freeze. Giant enters stage left, looking sad.)

Narrator/Old Man: The giant was very sad. A year passed and he began to realise he was very selfish. One day he saw one of the children under a tree crying and he went to help him.

(Giant mimes seeing the child. Nobody else can see him.)

Giant: Please, let me help. *(He reaches under the tree and mimes lifting up a child)* I have been a very selfish giant. I will open my garden up to everyone. *(He takes down the sign and exits.)*

Ice: Frost, I think he has learned his lesson.

Frost: It's time to go. I heard there is an ogre in Cornwall who hasn't been very nice.

Ice: Wind and Snow come on. It is time to go.

Snow: Do you have a map?

Frost: No! But I have my new Sat Nav.

Ice: Come on, let's go!

(They leave the stage.)

(One of the children spies a hole in the wall and climbs through. He calls the others.)

Fred: I can't believe we are inside the garden again!

Dick: It's spring time.

Billy: Winter has gone.

Cathy: And there's no notice. The giant's notice is gone!

Harry: And the garden is more beautiful than ever.

(The children hear the giant's footsteps and hide behind the trees. Giant comes on-stage and sees them. He waves them over. They are frightened but they move towards him slowly.)

Giant: Now I would like to join your games, if you please!!!! *(Suddenly looking around.)* But where is your little friend?

Anna: What are you talking about, sir?

Billy: Do you mean Fred over there?

Fred: He doesn't mean me. He means Dick. *(He pushes Dick forward.)*

Dick: Did you want something *(stuttering nervously)* Mmmmmister … ssssir … Mmmister … Fffffriendly … Giant?

Giant: I want to know where the little boy is, the one that I lifted up into the branches of the tree.

Ellie: But we haven't been in the garden since you put the sign up. Well not until today.

Fred: Then we heard your footsteps.

Anna: So we hid by the wall. I'm sorry that we trespassed in your garden, Mr. Giant.

(All apologize, suddenly worried that the giant might become selfish again.)

Giant: Oh no, no, no. You don't need to say sorry. I am the one who is sorry. Please think of this garden as yours now. But I wish you could tell me where the little child lives. I am very fond of him because it is through him that I realised I had been selfish with my garden. No wonder spring never came!

Ger: But this is all of us. No one else came with us.

Billy: But we will ask around in school tomorrow, and see if we can find out about your little friend.

Giant: Oh, yes, please. Now I really must have my rest. My old bones ache from all the playing. You carry on playing.

(Giant sits on the side of the stage and the children continue to play in slow motion.)

Narrator/Old Man: The years passed but the children were never able to find out who the giant's little friend had been. The giant grew very, very old. He could no longer play, so he sat in a huge armchair and watched the children. They all feared he would die soon.

(Giant mimes seeing the small child and calls out to him. Only Giant can see the small child. The children all stop playing immediately when they hear Giant talking. They look around but they can't see anyone.)

Giant: There he is! Come on, little friend. Where have you been? I've waited so long for you. Come and join in the fun. *(He hobbles towards the child)* My goodness, how I've missed you! I had a feeling I might die before you came to see me again.

(Giant moves to hug the child, and then draws back in horror as he takes the child's hands and examines them.)

Giant: Why, who has dared wound you? Tell me quickly, and I'll fetch my sword and kill him.

Small Child: *(Audience just hears the voice; they don't see small child, the voice can be done by the leader.)* No, these are the wounds of love.

Giant: *(Suddenly in awe.)* Who are you?

Small Child: Once you let me play in your garden. Today, you shall come with me to a very special garden called Paradise.

(Giant sinks slowly to the ground. The small child kneels beside the giant, makes him comfortable and comforts him. The children, aware Giant has died, sadly gather flowers and place them around him.)

The Land of the Trolls & Gargoyles

Cast of Characters (18): Jack, Sarah, Rover, 8 Gargoyles, Gargoyle Bob, 4 Trolls and 2 Friends.

(Stage Directions: there are cushions on the floor and a few chairs centre stage.)

Scene 1
(Jack comes in wearing a Superman outfit. He is chasing his dog, and starts tumbling and rolling around on the floor with him. His sister walks past him and raises her eyebrows up to heaven.)

Sarah: Jack, will you calm down? My friends are calling for me in a minute. I don't want them to see what a nutcase you are. No wonder Mum thinks you are naughty.

(Jack ignores her and continues playing with the dog. He thinks he is a dog as well.)

Sister: *(Getting very annoyed.)* Jack! Jack! Will you please stop? You are giving me a headache.

Jack: *(Still ignoring his sister and growling.)* Come on, Rover, let's makes a big massive fortress in the sand pit.

Rover: *(Gets excited, jumps up and down.)* Woof! Woof!

(Jack and Rover play with some cushions. Then they make a castle with the cushions. Sarah is cleaning up and sweeping the floor.)

Sarah: Is there any chance of you helping me tidy up? Mum will be back from work soon, and she will be very tired. You know she has been working so hard because she is frightened she might lose her job. *(Jack ignores her and continues building the cushion castle.)*

Sarah: JACK! JACK! Are you listening to me?

(She sighs and gives up when the phone rings.)

Sarah: *(On the phone.)* Oh My God, she didn't … What did he say? … I didn't show him anything ….

Jack: Rover, that's the best castle we have ever made. Let's get some soldiers to play with.

Sarah: *(Still on the phone.)* I can't believe it … he is so cute …oh my god ….

Jack: Hey, Sarah! Do you want to see the most amazing castle ever?

Sarah: *(Stops phone conversation.)* Mmmmmmm, let me think ... No! No! NO!

Jack: *(Looks dejectedly at Rover.)* What's wrong with her? We made it all by ourselves. *(Rubs Rover.)*

Rover: Woof! Woof! *(Doorbell rings and Sarah goes to answer it. Her two friends are there.)*

Sarah: Hi Girls. *(They air kiss one another.)*

Friend 1: Are you ready to go out?

Sarah: Nearly. I just have to wait for my mother to come home. I've to look after that wild thing.

Jack: Hey, do you want to see the most amazing thing ever?

Friend 2: Oh yeah, like a twerp like you can show us the most amazing thing ever.

Friend 1: We have seen a lot you know. We are 14 but show us what's so AMAZING! MAD JACK!

(The three girls laugh.)

Friend 1: MAD JACK! That's a perfect name for him.

(Jack shows them his castle. They all laugh at him.)

Friend 2: So that's the most AMAZING thing ever. (She knocks down his fort.) You are such a loser, MAD JACK!

Friend 1: Yeah, Loser. *(Makes L sign and knocks down the rest of the fort. Jack looks like he is going to cry.)*

Sarah: *(looks out the window)* Finally – my mother's back from work. Come on then. *(The girls run off stage left.)* Hi Mum, bye, Mum. Yes, I promise I will be back at 9 o'clock.

Jack: *(Hugs Rover.)* Girls can be so mean sometimes. We are lucky we are boys. Look at our lovely fortress. *(Goes to the left of the stage and shouts out.)* Hi Mum, when's dinner? I'm starving ... so is Rover.

Jack: Come on Rover let's play our favourite game – Gargoyles.

(Jack and Rover start going wild on the floor. They are tumbling and rolling around with each other.)

Jack: *(Shows his claws and growls.)* I'm going to eat you up.

Rover: Grrrrr. Woof!

(They are chasing each other around the stage when suddenly a very expensive ornament falls to the ground and breaks. Jack and Rover look shocked, and they stand still, with their mouths open. The stage goes black.)

End of Scene 1

Scene 2
(Front curtains are closed. Jack and the dog both come out to the front of the stage. Jack has been sent to his room.)

Jack: That was a very expensive ornament. We should have been more careful, Rover. We always get into trouble. We don't mean to be troublemakers, do we, Rover? *(Rover shakes his head.)* It's just that I love playing with you because you are my only friend. Mum is always working and Sarah has her own friends. Why does she want to be friends with those nasty girls anyway? *(Starts doing impressions of them.)* Oh My God you are so cool! He loves me so much… You are such a loser, Jack… Loser! Loser! Loser! … Mad Jack is such a loser… *(Looks at the ornament.)* Now we have been sent to bed without any dinner, Rover. We are stuck up here all night. We will be so bored. What can we do Rover? … I know, let's go where the Gargoyles are.

Rover: *(Looks confused.)* Woof!

Jack: Yes, all we need to do is jump into the wardrobe and go out the other side and then we will be in the Land of the Gargoyles.

Rover: *(Still looks confused.)* Woof! Woof!

Jack: Well, it worked for the children in *The Lion, the Witch and the Wardrobe*. They went through the wardrobe to get to Narnia. Why won't it work for us? Come on! Come on! Let's go on an amazing adventure.

(Jack turns and asks the audience.) Boys and girls, do you want to come with us through the wardrobe? *(He mimes going through the wardrobe.)*

End of Scene 2

Scene 3
(Curtains open. There is a boat centre stage made out of chairs, with a tree stage right. Jack and Rover see the boat. They jump in it and take off. They mime pulling up the mast and getting tangled in the ropes, but then they get the sail up. They go faster and faster. Play "Titanic" music. This can be a movement and mime sequence if there is no boat.)

Jack: Look, Rover, there is a beach and a huge jungle behind it.

Rover: I'm scared. I want to go home.

Jack: I thought you were a dog not a cat. Scaredy cat! Scaredy cat!

(They land on shore and get out. They are very cautious, especially Rover. They move to the right of the stage. They hear something coming, so they hide behind a tree.)

(Three gargoyles come on from stage left. They are dancing and thrashing about – destroying everything in sight.)

Gargoyle 1: I'm bored. I want to go home.

Gargoyle 3: That's going to be difficult because you have managed to get us lost. Yet again!

Gargoyle 1: But I saw something. I promise I did. It was over there. *(Points stage left.)*

Gargoyle 2: You are always seeing things.

Gargoyle 1: Oh, be quiet. Look! Look! Over there. It is a boat. Someone has sailed to our island.

Gargoyle 2: I'm scared. Shouldn't we go home and tell the others?

Gargoyle 3: Sssssssssssssssssssshhhhhhhhhhhhhhh

(He sneaks around looking under everything like trees and plants and then he finds both Rover and Jack. Rover starts crying.)

Rover: I think the monsters are going to eat us.

Jack: Don't be ridiculous. Just watch this.

(Jack runs, shouts and jumps up and down, trying to scare the gargoyles. When they see how little he is they start to circle Jack and Rover.)

Rover: Look, they are massive. Look at the size of their teeth.

Gargoyle 2: They are tiny. *(They peer down at Jack and Rover.)*

Gargoyle 3: We could eat them for lunch.

Gargoyle 1: I'm feeling a bit peckish.

Gargoyle 2: Shall we eat them then?

Rover: Please don't eat us!

Gargoyle 3: Yes, let's eat them.

Jack: Be still everyone.

(The gargoyles freeze.)

Jack: Don't anyone move!

Gargoyles: Why?

Jack: Because I am your King. I am King of the Gargoyles, and this is Rover my loyal servant. From now on you will listen to ME.

Gargoyles: *(They bend down on one knee.)* Oh yes, Master!

Gargoyle 1: Is he really the king?

Gargoyle 2: Yes he is.

Gargoyle 3: He is a bit too small to be the king, isn't he?

Gargoyle 1: Well, legend has it that the King of the Gargoyles would arrive here in a boat.

Gargoyle 2: Welcome, Your Majesty. Welcome to our humble abode.

Jack: Thank you.

Gargoyle 3: Come with us. We will take you to our gargoyle campsite, and you can meet some of the other gargoyles.

Jack: Take us to your people, and I will show you how to be real people.

(Exit stage left and curtains close)

End of Scene 3

Scene 4
(Curtains open. They all arrive at the campsite of the gargoyles. All the other gargoyles come to greet them. They are bashing into each other and falling over.)

Gargoyle 1: Hey, everyone! Hail the KING of the GARGOYLES!!!

Gargoyle 2: Hail, oh King.

(Everyone bows. One gargoyle comes and gives Jack a crown and sceptre and places the crown on his head.)

Jack: Okay, everyone, let's party!

(Music comes on and everyone thrashes and rolls around the stage. This could be a dance where the audience can join in.)

Gargoyle 4: I'm so glad he's here.

Gargoyle 5: Yes, I am too.

Gargoyle 6: He looks a bit small to be King.

Gargoyle 7: He looks a bit small to help us with the trolls.

Gargoyle 4: So, King Jack, how are you going to protect us from the trolls?

Jack: Who are the trolls?

Gargoyle 5: They live on the other side of the island. They like to fight with us all the time.

Gargoyle 6: They want to defeat us so they can stop us making noise and having fun.

Gargoyle 7: Yes, they are such horrible monsters.

Rover: *(Whispers to Jack)* Now I'm scared. Can't we just get back into the boat and go home?

Jack: Don't be silly, Rover. We can defeat the trolls. We are the gargoyles.

(All the gargoyles cheer.)

Gargoyles: Three cheers for King Jack! Hip, hip hooray! Hip, hip hooray! Hip, hip hooray!

Jack: I have a wonderful idea. We will build an amazing fortress. It will be one of the most amazing fortresses you have ever seen. We will put a moat around it and no one will ever come and stop us from having fun. We can be gargoyles every day. We can have lots of tunnels in it, so that we can hide from the trolls.

Gargoyle 8: We need to call for Gog then?

Jack and Rover: Who is Gog?

Gargoyle 8: Why, Gog the Builder, of course.

(Get the audience to shout for Gog. Gog comes up from the audience. He is a gargoyle, but he has a toolkit around his waist.)

Gog: What's all the commotion about?

Gargoyle 1: King Jack wants us to build a fortress to keep the trolls out.

Gargoyle 2: Yes, and it's going to have a moat around it.

Gog: Okay then, we'd better get started.

(The gargoyles, Jack and Rover mime building a fortress.)

End of Scene 4

Scene 5
(Four trolls come on stage and stand at the front. They point at the audience and look angry. The gargoyles are at the back of the stage, miming building a fortress. The trolls start asking the audience where all the noise is coming from. They accuse the audience of making the noise.)

Troll 1: What's all this noise?

Troll 2: *(Points to the audience)* Look, it must be them.

Troll 3: *(Asks the audience)* Is it you, boys and girls?

(Audience denies that they are making noise.)

Troll 1: I knew it couldn't be them. *(Points at the audience.)*

Troll 2: Yes, they are too small.

Troll 3: Well if it's not them it must be those horrible gargoyles.

Troll 4: They think they are great just because they have a new king.

Troll 1: How do you know that?

Troll 4: I read it in the *Daily Gargoyle*.

Troll 2: That old tabloid.

Troll 4: That King Jack looks a bit small though.

Troll 3: Yes, we will be able to defeat him easily.

(The trolls are hit by rolled up pieces of paper – hailstones.)

Troll 1: Ow! What was that?

Troll 2: Oh, stop complaining. You do nothing but complain! … Ow!

Troll 3: We are being pelted by snowballs!

Troll 4: Where are they coming from?

Troll 1: Look over there! From that fortress.

Trolls: Quick, run!

(They run off stage. All the gargoyles start laughing and also leave the stage.)

End of Scene 5

Scene 6
(The trolls enter from stage left. They look very tired.)

Troll 1: That was a close shave.

Troll 2: Those gruesome gargoyles.

Troll 3: *(Speaks to the audience.)* We don't like them do we boys and girls?

Troll 4: Let's hope we get a good night's sleep.

Troll 1: Boys and girls, you let us know if the gargoyles turn up.

(They all lie down and go to sleep.)

(The gargoyles come up through the tunnels from below the stage. They put their fingers to their lips and make faces at the audience, asking the boys and girls to be quiet; then the gargoyles tickle the trolls and run away.)

(They repeat this two more times.)

Trolls: Okay, we give up.

Troll 1: If we can't beat you, we will join you.

Gargoyle 1: All bow for His Majesty, King of the Gargoyles – King Jack.

(Trumpet blows and Jack enters with Rover by his side. All the gargoyles and trolls bow.)

Gargoyle 2: Boys and girls, you need to bow, too.

Jack: Well, Trolls, do you want to be gargoyles now?

Trolls: Oh yes, please.

Jack: *(He puts his sword on their shoulders, one-by-one.)* I now pronounce you a wild thing.

(Everyone cheers and music plays. Everyone goes off stage except Jack and Rover.)

Rover: That was amazing. I can't believe you pulled it off. You really are King of the Gargoyles now. This is a great place. We can have fun here every day.

(Jack doesn't say anything; he looks very sad.)

Rover: What's the matter, Jack?

Jack: I've had enough of this place. I want to go home – to my own house, my own bed, my own family.

Rover: Well, we could just hop on the boat and make our way home if that's what you really want to do.

Jack: There is the boat. Come on quickly.

(They both run off stage.)

(Gargoyles come back on stages, with the trolls, all having a great time.)

Gargoyle 1: Where's King Jack?

Troll 1: Look! Look! Over there in the distance I see them in their boat.

Gargoyle and Trolls: Bye, King Jack. Bye, Rover. We will miss you.

Troll 3: So what are we going to play now?

(They all skip off-stage playing with one another.)

End of Scene 6

Scene 7
(Jack and Rover walk onto a dark stage.)

Jack: Oh, at last we are home.

(Rover wags his tail and gets excited.)

Jack: Someone is coming. Can you hear footsteps?

Rover: Woof!

(The door opens and Sarah comes in.)

Jack: Oh Sarah! I've missed you. Have you missed me?

Sarah: *(Looks confused.)* I've been out with my friends … but, yes, Twerp, I've missed you. Mum says come downstairs for a hot chocolate. All that rushing around must have made you thirsty. I think she wants a cuddle as well.

Jack: Okay. Come on, Rover, let's go, Geronimoooooooooooooooooooo.

(Jack storms off stage.)

Sarah: *(Looks at the audience.)* Some things never change.

The End

No Excuse

Cast of Characters (11): Four Children, Four Bullies, Victim, Mother, Father

(Stage Directions: the stage is set up with the four children sitting very close together centre stage, in four chairs which should be almost overlapping. Have two in front and two in back, but not directly behind the ones in front. As each child says their part, they can change positions, but at any given time, each should be in a different position, i.e. one standing, one sitting, one slouching, etc. The other action takes place stage left and stage right.)

Child 1: It wasn't supposed to end up like this. I mean, I didn't really mean for this to happen. In fact, if you really look at the situation, you'll see that it wasn't my fault at all. I wasn't even involved. There is this guy at my school. Kind of a weird guy. Doesn't quite fit in, if you know what I mean. He's the kind of guy that keeps to himself and does his own thing. I never bothered him. I never really thought all that much about him. He was just there. And I was doing my own thing.

Child 1 and 2: It wasn't really my fault at all.

Child 2: It wasn't my idea. I just went along with it because my friends were. They thought that it would be funny to mess with this one guy at school. They just thought that if they broke into his locker and stole his phone, we could all get a good laugh out of it. It wasn't a big deal at all. I didn't really even do anything,

(Narrators freeze. Stage left, four bullies are standing in front of a locker.)

Bully 1: Quick, hurry.

Bully 2: Come on, will you.

Bully 3: I am going as fast as I can.

Bully 4: Look, we got it.

Bully 1: Hmm, don't look now, but guess who is here.

Victim: What are you doing?

Bully 2: Stealing your phone. What are you going to do about it?

(Bully 3 pushes Victim to the ground.)

Bully 4: We are taking your phone and you are not to say anything.

(Four bullies and Victim freeze for a moment and then all walk quietly off-stage.)

Child 3: I don't know why children pick on me. I'm really not all that different. I just like to keep to myself. I don't feel like talking to a lot of children. I guess I'm kind of distracted when I'm at school. I have a lot of stuff going on at home, you know? And so I think about it a lot. It's hard to focus on everyone having fun when I've got so much stress at home. I'm not trying to be anti-social or anything. I just have a lot on my mind.

(Narrators freeze. Stage right, Father is sleeping in the corner with a bottle. Victim is watching telly. Mother comes into the room.)

Mother: Look at the state of him. How long has he been like that?

Victim: Since I got home from school.

Mother: Wake up, you silly fool.

Father: *(wakes and grunts)* Shut up, you stupid cow.

(They have a fight. Father starts to hit Mother, then everyone freezes. Father/Mother walk off-stage and Victim freezes.)

Child 4: I really hate my school, though. Children there are just so juvenile and unfocused. It really brings me down. I have a hard time focusing there, and I don't want to make trouble for myself.

(Child 4 moves stage right and stands beside Victim.)

Victim: Do you want to go into town after school? I don't want to go home.

Child 4: No offence. I'd like to, but I don't think I should be seen with you.

Victim: Why not?

Child 4: Because they might start on me then, and I really don't want that.

(Child 4 moves back to his chair, centre stage.)

Child 4: They just kept picking on him. Every day there is something new – new signs on his locker, new nicknames for him. They just never let up. I didn't think that it was my place to say anything. I mean, I wasn't involved. I don't even know him that well.

Child 3: I just need someone to listen to me. I don't want them to fix my problems or even tell me what to do. I just want someone to listen; someone to help me sort through everything that is in my head so that I don't have to carry it all alone. It's hard to be so alone all the time.

Child 2: So we put stuff in his locker, right? Like a dead mouse. And he didn't do anything about it. He doesn't get mad, doesn't fight back. It's as if he doesn't even notice that we did anything. Well, it gets all of the lads really mad because they wanted to get at least some kind of rise out of this kid. So they devise even crazier stuff to get at him. I didn't really think it was a good idea. I mean, this kid never did anything to any of us. But you can't just say something like that to your friends. I mean, they'd think I was afraid or something, and I didn't want that to happen. So I just let it go.

(Four children freeze centre stage.)

(Stage right: Victim opens his locker, sighs and throws the mouse in the bin and freezes. Four bullies are watching.)

Bully 1: What is his problem?

Bully 2: Dunno.

Bully 3: We just have to think of something better.

Bully 4: Like what?

(Four bullies freeze.)

Child 1: I figured that a leader would step in or something. If it got too bad, someone would do something. And so I didn't need to worry about it. I wasn't doing anything wrong, so I should just stay out of it. Besides, these guys wouldn't do anything too bad, right? I mean, they would stop before it got out of hand. It always stops before it gets out of hand.

Child 4: They are so out of hand at my school. Everyone swears all the time and all anyone can talk about is getting drunk. I don't do any of that stuff, of course. They have no excuse to be acting the way that they do.

Child 3: They just kept at me. I tried to ignore them, but they just kept on going. It was like the more that I ignored them the more they decided to pick on me.

(Narrators freeze and action moves stage right again.)

Victim: Why won't you just leave me alone? I just want to be left alone.

Bully 2: Oh, come on. You're such a stupid little boy. Why won't you fight like a man?

Victim: I don't want to fight you.

Bully 1: Why? Are you scared?

(Victim and four bullies go off-stage.)

(Centre stage – Child 3 is now sitting down with his back to the audience, head down.)

Child 1 and 2: No one was supposed to get hurt.

Child 1: This wasn't supposed to happen. Someone was supposed to stop it. There is no way that this should have happened here. A leader should have stopped this.

Child 4: I knew that something like this would happen. I should have helped him, but I didn't. I was too concerned with not been bullied myself.

Child 1: My excuse is that someone else was going to stop all of this.

Child 2: My excuse is that it was only a laugh. Nobody was meant to get hurt.

Child 4: My excuse is that I had to look after myself.

Child 1/2/4: My excuse is …

(As this last line is said, Child 3 gets up and walks off-stage. Everyone else freezes.)

The Boy Who Cried Wolf

Cast of Characters (26): Six storytellers, six sheep, six wolves, six townspeople, shepherd boy, his father.

(The shepherd boy is sitting on a chair centre stage; the sheep are all around him, grazing in the field. Townspeople and boy's father are stage left, miming working, and the wolves are stage right, asleep.)

Storyteller 1: Once upon a time, there was a young shepherd boy.

Storyteller 2: He lived in a lonely valley, next to a great, dark forest.

Storyteller 3: He had to look after his father's sheep and protect them from the wolves that lived in the forest.

Storyteller 4: It was a lonely job, and the boy was bored.

(Boy starts to yawn and stretch.)

Storyteller 5: He wanted some fun and action.

Storyteller 6: One day …

Shepherd Boy: Oh boy! I'm so bored! There is nothing to do!

Sheep: Baa! Baa! Baa!

Sheep 1: Why are you so bored?

Sheep 2: Yes, you can play with us.

Sheep 3: We always have fun following each other.

Sheep 4: Don't you like us?

Shepherd Boy: Yes, but I'm bored. I want to be in the village playing with my friends!

Sheep 5: I have an idea if you want some excitement.

Shepherd Boy and other sheep: WHAT?

Sheep 5: Pretend there is a wolf attacking all the sheep.

Sheep 6: Don't listen to him. He *(points to sheep 5)* is always causing trouble.

Shepherd Boy: No, it is a brilliant plan. Let's do it right now. *(Boy goes stage left and shouts.)* Wolf! Wolf! Help! The mean, old wolf is coming.

(His father and townspeople run toward centre stage with shotguns, sticks and shovels as the sheep run off-stage.)

Storyteller 1: His father and the townspeople came rushing to help him.

Father: Where's the wolf?

Townsperson 1: Where did he go?

Townsperson 2: I'll get him.

Townsperson 3: Did you see the wolf?

Townsperson 4: Did he go back to the forest?

Townsperson 5: Has he killed our sheep?

Shepherd Boy: False alarm! False alarm! I thought I saw the wolf, but it must have been a shadow.

Townsperson 6: False alarm. Let's go home.

(Exit father and the townspeople. The sheep return, laughing. The boy sits on his chair laughing and the sheep gather around him.)

Storyteller 2: This excitement pleased the shepherd boy.

Storyteller 3: It made him laugh and clap his hands.

(Boy laughs and claps his hands.)

Storyteller 4: A few days later, he tried the same trick again.

Storyteller 5: This time the sheep didn't know that it was a trick.

Shepherd Boy: Wolf! Wolf! The mean, old wolf is coming.

(Sheep scatter off-stage. Enter father and townspeople with shotguns, sticks and shovels.)

Father: Good lad! Tell us where the wolf is!

Townspeople: Did he go this way or that way?

Townsperson 1: He won't get far.

Townsperson 2: We could follow his tracks.

Townsperson 3: But there aren't any paw prints.

Townsperson 4: Where's the wolf?

Shepherd Boy: False alarm! False alarm! I thought I saw the wolf. It must have been a shadow again.

Townspeople 5 & 6: False alarm! Let's go home again.

(Townspeople leave and the sheep come back, but this time they are relieved.)

Sheep: YOU FRIGHTENED US.

Shepherd Boy: Hee! Hee! Hee!

Storyteller 6: The boy played the trick several more times. Then one day the shepherd boy thought he saw something big and furry moving in the woods.

(Boy looks towards the wolves but shakes his head and goes to sleep with the sheep. Wolves start slinking towards the centre of the stage.)

Wolf 1: Have you seen this?

Wolf 2: What?

Wolf 3: Lots and lots of sheep.

Wolf 4: Where are they?

Wolf 5: Are you blind?

Wolf 6: Look over there!

(Points to the sheep and the boy who are all asleep.)

Wolf 4: Oh, yes, now I see them.

Wolf 1: Sssh, be quiet.

Wolf 2: We could have a very good dinner tonight.

Wolf 3: You mean for the rest of week.

Wolf 5: The boy is by himself.

Wolf 6: Yes. No one is there to help him. Quick, let's go.

Shepherd Boy: I thought I saw something, but it is only a shadow. *(Yawns.)* I think I'll have another little nap.

(Wolves come to centre stage and prowl around dramatically, gesturing to the audience to be quiet. Then they grab a sheep each.)

Wolves: We are mean, old wolves with a bad reputation. It's time to eat a juicy sheep for our dinner.

Sheep: Baa! Baa! Baa!

Storyteller 1: The shepherd boy woke up!

Shepherd Boy: AHHHH. Help! Wolf! Wolf! The mean, old wolves are here!

Storyteller 2: He called and called but no one came.

(His father and townspeople are stage left, miming working.)

Storyteller 3: They were fed up with his lies.

Storyteller 4: The wolves took all the sheep.

Storyteller 5: The moral of the story is …

Storyteller 6: … nobody believes a liar, even when they are telling the truth.